Church Growth 101

Church Growth 101
A Church Growth Guidebook
for Ministers and Laity

Dr. Glenn W. Mollette

Newburgh Press
Newburgh, Indiana
United States of America

For Carole.
Thanks for reading, editing and your loving support!

More than half of this book was written when my
sons were very young. Thank you Jared and Zachary
for all that you gave so dad could serve as a pastor.

In Memory
Rev. James H. Grayson (Brother Jimmy)
My pastor who modeled personal evangelism.

Table of Contents

Chapter 1

Vision

> *"Where there is no vision the people perish…"*
> ~ *Proverbs 29:18*

Vision begins with calling. Saul had one vision for his life. Then, he met Jesus on the Damascus road and his life's calling was totally changed. ~*Acts 9:3-9* Saul was called by Jesus. He spent the rest of his life following the Lord's calling on his life.

That calling took Saul throughout the world to tell others about Jesus. All who met the man called Saul, who became the Apostle Paul, were changed. No one could meet Paul without hearing about Jesus. Jesus was the passion of his life.

Christ's calling upon Paul's life became the vision of his life. All that he saw and wanted to do was centered in Christ. Paul would go on to experience the problems and pressures of his service for Christ. There would be a lot of heartache along the way. Yet, because of Paul's calling and internal drive to live for Christ and follow Him he would say, "…I know whom I have believed, and am persuaded that he is able to keep that which I have committed unto him against that day." ~*2 Timothy 1:12*

Paul would write, "I have fought a good fight, I have finished my course, I have kept the faith:" ~*2 Timothy 4:7*

Calling is not easy to explain, but it's easy to feel, see and experience. We read about how Paul changed and how he lived the rest of his life. We see how God used him throughout the book of Acts and then in his other New Testament writings.

We read about Moses standing at the burning bush in *Exodus*, *chapter three*. Hearing the call of God he led God's people out of Egypt and was with them for forty years in the desert.

Peter was called by Jesus to follow Him. During Christ's final hour Peter was struggling. We read about him denying Christ and weeping. ~*Mark 14:66-72* After the resurrection of Jesus we read about an empowered Peter preaching on the day of Pentecost and over three thousand coming to Christ. ~*Acts 2* Peter's demeanor completely changed when he saw his risen Savior.

The strength of life is in our internal drive. Everything we are and do begins internally. Our desire to walk with God, serve Him and live for Him begins internally. Our life follows the direction of our mind. I've heard it said a hundred times "Sow a thought, reap an act; sow an act, reap a life; sow a life, reap a destiny."

The life and destiny begin with our thinking. Our thinking is wrapped up in what or who controls or impresses us. The life can be taken in any direction that the mind and heart lead it or propel it to go. Once the mind formulates the thought, then it can be acted upon or dismissed.

Acting upon a thought may take hours, weeks or even years to generate the action behind the thought. You may think about buying a house. The thought becomes a passion and the passion helps you to formulate a vision for how to fulfill the passion. In most cases, it will take years of work, saving enough money for a down payment and then working for fifteen to thirty years to pay for the house. The vision of owning the house and someday having it completely paid for will drive you to stay the course with the monthly payments in anticipation of the result.

Most people get very tired of the agonizing monthly payments and long for the day when the last payment will be made. They have a vision of reaching the day when they know it is paid in full.

The internal drive fuels the vision. We don't want to go hungry, so we work to buy food. We don't enjoy walking everywhere we go, so we work to purchase a car. We don't want to sleep in the streets, so we also work to provide shelter. The thought of being homeless or financially broke is not appealing. Internally, our thinking is stirred to prevent that kind of life event from happening. Our thinking formulates a vision for how we might buy food and provide for the other necessities of life.

The internal drive is inspired or motivated by what we see and hear. We see God working in the lives of others. We hear the message of Christ and it is good news to our hearts. This good news moves us to think about God and our relationship to Him. Our thinking is expressed by action as we confess Him as Lord and Savior, follow Him in baptism and unite with a church fellowship. We study His Word, hear it preached and see Christ working in the lives of others and soon we begin to formulate other thoughts about our relationship to Christ and how we might personally do and be more for Him.

Our internal drive is where God continues His work of calling us. It is in our hearts and minds that God speaks to us and we know that we must do something for Him that is beyond the ordinary. This calling takes men and women to places they have never been before.

From this internal thinking comes external living. We become what we think about. If we think about how we might live for and serve God then that's what we will do. The vision for life begins internally. Where there is good thinking there will be good living. Good living is the result of good thinking.

Church growth begins with the thought. The thought develops a plan, a vision and a burning desire to bring it about.

God reaches out to us in the power of His Spirit. We have His Spirit because we have Christ within us. Paul wrote in *Galatians* 2:20, "I have been crucified with Christ; and it is no longer I that live, but Christ living in me: and that life which I now live in the flesh I live in faith, the faith which is in the Son of God, who loved me, and gave Himself up for me".

Paul's faith, his thinking and his lifestyle are wrapped around Christ. His life direction was changed. God changes our life direction.

Life is greater because of the purpose, peace, power and progression that we experience as we walk with God. In *2 Timothy 1:12*, I believe we read about Paul's personal relationship with Christ and with others. We read about his passion for serving Jesus as well as the pressure that came with his service. Even more, we read about the peace that dwelled in Paul's life.

In Christ, we realize there is more beyond the grave and this world. God saves, calls us and implants the vision. There is the vision to live in fellowship with Him, enjoy Him, serve Him and follow His leading in our lives.

Christ gives us a new heart. We are new creations. "Wherefore if any man is in Christ, he is a new creature: the old things are passed away; behold, they are become new." *~2 Corinthians 5:17*

The relationship we have with Christ will help us with the following:

1. We Can – "I can do all things through Christ which strengtheneth me." *~Philippians 4:13*

2. We Must – If we can, then we must. If God strengthens us, then we must. "What shall we then say to these things? If God be for us, who can be against us? He that spared not his own Son, but delivered him up for us all, how shall he not with him also freely give us all things?" *~Romans 8:31-32*

3. Why Not? - If you can and God can, then why not? "For with God nothing shall be impossible." *~Luke 1:37*

4. The Power of Trying – Most won't try. When you try, you are doing what most people will not consider. Failure is simply

when we will not try. "Let us not become weary in doing good, for at the proper time we will reap a harvest if we do not give up." *~Galatians 6:9 NIV*

5. Success Comes by Staying with It – "Let us not become weary in doing good, for at the proper time we will reap a harvest if we do not give up" *~Galatians 6:9 NIV* Church growth, a long marriage, a savings account, retiring from a job; most everything worthwhile involves time and staying with it.

6. Age – We have to get over age. Don't worry about being too young or too old. Age is always changing. In *1 Timothy 4:12 NIV*, Paul told Timothy, "Don't let anyone look down on you because you are young, but set an example for the believers in speech, in conduct, in love, in faith and in purity." Then we read in *Joshua 14:6-13* about Caleb who was 85 and God was still using him in a great way.

7. A Negative Person Never Will – The negative person is relying on everything but God. The Bible says, "I can do all things through Christ which strengtheneth me." *~Philippians 4:13.* A church committee was arguing about the impossibilities of expanding the church. Two little boys were walking down the hall and heard the committee arguing. In childlike faith one said, "God can do anything." The other said, "If you are going to bring God into it that changes everything."

8. Walk with God – "Enoch walked with God..." *~Genesis 5:24*

9. It Begins with the Thought - "For as he thinketh in his heart so is he:" *~Proverbs 23:7* Our thinking leads us. A church begins with the seed of a thought. A soul is won to Christ with the seed of one thought – compassion for the lost soul. A song is written with a thought and an idea. A sermon, a book and a lifestyle begin with one thought.

10. Love God and Live with a Grateful Attitude – "For God so loved the world, that he gave his only begotten Son, that

whosoever believeth in Him should not perish, but have
everlasting life." ~*John 3:16* It does not get any better than
this verse in the Bible.

Our life and service for Him recognizes that He loves us and that
everything we have comes from Him. We live with a daily attitude
of gratitude for the life God has given us. We thank and praise Him
for every opportunity of living our life for Him. *Psalm 107:1 NIV*
says, "Give thanks to the Lord, for he is good: His loves endures
forever."

Only one life, soon will be passed, only what is done for Christ
will last.

Four Characteristics of Church Health

The key to church growth is health. A healthy church will grow.
The church where the body of Christ is functioning as His body and
Christ is the head will have a right heart. The membership with a
right heart can solve most any problem. They will also attract new
people to their church. People want to attend where there is a good
atmosphere. You can't hide a good atmosphere. It is not artificially
created. It is in the minds and hearts of the people attending.

In a healthy church four characteristics abound:
1. Love abounds
2. Forgiveness abounds
3. Help abounds
4. Inclusiveness abounds

~*1 Corinthians chapters 12-13*

Chapter 2

Connecting People to God and Man

There seems to always be another program, seminar or book offering a plan for church growth. The best plan is the one that works for you and your church. There is not a proven program that works the same way for every situation. What works at one church may not necessarily work at another.

People have to feel connected. The church that will help people feel connected to God and others will have a growing congregation. Jesus said in *Luke 10:27 NIV*, " He answered: 'Love the Lord your God with all your heart and with all your soul and with all your strength and with all your mind'; and, 'Love your neighbor as yourself.'"

It is vital to be in relationship with God and with people. We need God and we need people. Christ has made it possible by His death on the Cross and resurrection from the grave to connect us in relationship with God. By our salvation, through faith in Jesus as our personal Savior, our hearts and lives become connected to the omnipotent triune holy God almighty.

Jesus came and paid a heavy price. He paid for our salvation by His death on the cross. He gave His blood to cleanse us of our sins. He made it possible for us to have access to God and live in a daily relationship with Him through His Son Jesus.

"But God demonstrates his own love for us in this: While we were still sinners, Christ died for us." ~*Romans 5.8 NIV*

The greatest gift we have is to know and feel we are connected to a loving, forgiving, powerful heavenly father. We need God. People want to know and feel that they are connected to Him.

Conversion comes through connection. Conversion is turning from sin and turning to God. It is repentance from an old life but turning to Christ for a new life. The change is inward.

Someone introduces you to Christ. Possibly a parent, a sibling, a child, a preacher, teacher or a friend introduces you to Christ. They invite you to church. They talk to you about a relationship with God. They give you a gospel tract. Someone takes you to a good church where you hear the story preached about a loving God. A growing church is people connecting other people to Jesus.

Conversion leads to commitment. If the church is filled with people who have never experienced conversion then the church will be overwhelmingly uncommitted. It will also be a church that is overwhelmingly lost.

The church that has lost people in leadership will act like a lost organization. There will be internal fighting, pouting, dishonesty, jockeying for a place of leadership just like people act in non-church social organizations.

Lost people do not financially support the church. They may give a few token gifts along the way, but remember they aren't committed. God does not have their hearts. When God does not have your heart you aren't going to give much. Often, these are the most vocal people in the church. They make the most noise, if given the opportunity, but produce the least. They can't produce anything because there is nothing really within them. They have not truly been converted to Christ in faith.

Conversion to Christ leads to a committed life to Christ in heart and our life actions.

> "Therefore, if any man be in Christ, he is a new creature: old
> things are passed away; behold, all things are become new."
> ~2 Corinthians 5:17

Commitment brings a feeling of completeness. People stagger through life today looking for the missing piece of the puzzle. We find fulfillment in family, friends, work, money, houses, cars, other relationships, hobbies and temporary obsessions. Nothing will bring ultimate completeness until we are focused on Christ and our hearts are settled on Him. We can do many things, work in ten different directions in our daily living but our anchor is in Christ. He is the solid rock on which we stand.

The growing church is helping people to find completion in Christ as they are connecting people to God.

As Christians, church helps us feel more connected to God in different ways. It begins at the front door of the church. It is powerful to have five to ten people in the entrance area of the church welcoming people. It is a drag to walk into a church and the entrance area is empty. Possibly the Sunday bulletin is visibly placed for you to pick up as you enter the sanctuary but there is no one to welcome you.

A number of smiling, happy people, offering a handshake and a welcome sets the beginning stage of how you will feel in the hour of worship. When we go to church it is nice to feel welcomed. It helps when those doing the greeting not only shake hands but say "Hello or good morning. What is your name? Where are you from? It's great to have you with us today." The person who hears this immediately thinks, "These people are nice." There is an internal boost to the person who is visiting the church. The thought is, "I'm welcome here." This is huge if you are going to grow your church.

If you don't want to grow, don't care about people and you won't. Do not put the most unpleasant people you have out front welcoming people. A few pleasant people who can smile and welcome others are effective. "A cheerful heart is a good medicine; But a broken spirit drieth up the bones." *~Proverbs 17:22*

The average person, walking into the doors of the church, needs this good medicine. Inject them at the front door with smiles, happy faces and happy hearts. After all, it is church and Jesus has changed us. There is much about life that can crush our spirits, but we are in Christ and He has given us the victory over those things in life that are crushing. The Bible says, "We are hard pressed on every side, but not crushed; perplexed, but not in despair; persecuted, but not abandoned; struck down, but not destroyed. We always carry around in our body the death of Jesus, so that the life of Jesus may also be revealed in our body." ~2 Corinthians 4:8-10 NIV

At the entry area of the church we have a great opportunity to reveal the life of Jesus. We reveal Him in our face, our body, our posture, and our disposition. We do not want the saddest face in the welcoming lobby of the church. We do not want to inject people with unhappiness and sourness before they enter the sanctuary or Bible study for worship.

Often this will spill over into the congregation. If a gracious and happy spirit starts at the front door, then there is a chance it will be carried over into the congregational attitude.

The congregation's attitude is important. Smile and shake hands with the people around you. Offer to move over and make room for people when they come into the worship area. This is all very uncontrollable. Churches develop and maintain this personality or they don't. The church that does has a better chance of growing. When you go to church you want to feel like those sitting around you are happy that you are there.

People are connected to God by music. Music is powerful. Music speaks to our hearts and moves us emotionally. Music helps us celebrate a loving God and a risen Savior. Music can help us feel the love and forgiveness of God. Music helps bring us out of despair so that we can have peace in our lives. "Praise him with the timbrel and dance: praise him with stringed instruments and organs." ~Psalm 150:4

Unfortunately, if the music is bad, it may turn us the other way. Bad music does not enhance great worship. Of course, we always

give high marks to the singers and musicians who love God and
are trying to do something for Him. There is the scriptural truth of
"Make a joyful noise unto the Lord..." *~Psalm 100:1*

The challenge today is that most everybody listens to some music
on the television, radio, or other electronic devices. Often the only
live music that people hear during the week will be at the church.
Too many times, church choirs have just thrown something together
for Sunday worship. We need to do the best we can.

Churches that are growing today pay close attention to the music.
Musicians, praise teams, ensembles and well rehearsed choirs greatly
impact the mood of the worship. A good praise team with two or
three musicians can set the tone for the opening of the worship
service. This music simply needs to be Christ exalting and well
rehearsed and you need to select music that connects man to God.

Prayer – Give people a chance to pray on Sunday. The minds of
average people are filled with the events of life. While many may be
celebrating the victories and achievements of their lives, others are
battling disappointments, suffering grief, negative medical reports
and fears about family and life.

People need to hear and feel God at work. When we pray, we
bring God into it. When God is a part of what we are experiencing,
we feel better about what is going on. Give a special place to prayer
in your time of worship.

Samuel spoke to Israel at Saul's coronation in the Old Testament
saying "Do not be afraid, Samuel replied. You have done all this
evil; yet do not turn away from the LORD, but serve the LORD
with all your heart. Do not turn away after useless idols. They can
do you no good, nor can they rescue you, because they are useless.
For the sake of his great name the LORD will not reject his people,
because the LORD was pleased to make you his own. As for me,
far be it from me that I should sin against the LORD by failing to
pray for you. And I will teach you the way that is good and right."

~1 Samuel 12:20-23 NIV Samuel, a man greatly used of God, understood the importance of prayer.

The Gospel of *Luke 11:1-13* says, "And it came to pass, that, as he was praying in a certain place, when he ceased, one of his disciples said unto him, Lord, teach us to pray, as John also taught his disciples.

And he said unto them, When ye pray, say, Our Father which art in heaven, Hallowed be thy name. Thy kingdom come. Thy will be done, as in heaven, so in earth. Give us day by day our daily bread. And forgive us our sins; for we also forgive every one that is indebted to us. And lead us not into temptation; but deliver us from evil.

And he said unto them, Which of you shall have a friend, and shall go unto him at midnight, and say unto him, Friend, lend me three loaves; For a friend of mine in his journey is come to me, and I have nothing to set before him?

And he from within shall answer and say, Trouble me not: the door is now shut, and my children are with me in bed; I cannot rise and give thee.

I say unto you, Though he will not rise and give him, because he is his friend, yet because of his importunity he will rise and give him as many as he needeth.

And I say unto you, Ask, and it shall be given you; seek, and ye shall find; knock, and it shall be opened unto you. For every one that asketh receiveth; and he that seeketh findeth; and to him that knocketh it shall be opened.

If a son shall ask bread of any of you that is a father, will he give him a stone? or if he ask a fish, will he for a fish give him a serpent? Or if he shall ask an egg, will he offer him a scorpion?

If ye then, being evil, know how to give good gifts unto your children: how much more shall your heavenly Father give the Holy Spirit to them that ask him."

Jesus prayed, knew the importance of prayer and taught his

disciples to pray. The prayer time is major in our worship service.

Give people a chance to focus and kneel at the front of the church or by their seat or pew. Prayer is talking to God. There is expression in prayer. Heart-felt powerful praying will have powerful results in our lives.

The Scriptures – Read the Bible in church. The singing, preaching, praying and all that we do must be centered in God's Word if the worship is going to have an impact. The Word points us to Jesus and tells us how life is to be lived. The Bible should be read at every service. "The grass withers and the flowers fall, but the word of our God endures forever." *~Isaiah 40:8 NIV* "Jesus answered, 'It is written: Man does not live on bread alone, but on every word that comes from the mouth of God.'" *~Matthew 4:4 NIV*

Preaching – The sermon portion of worship is contingent on the deliverer, how it is being delivered and what is being delivered. Great preaching comes from a heart that is right with God. If the preacher's heart is wrong, then everything said has little impact. A right heart is a heart at peace with God, clear from any obstruction. If the heart and mind of the preacher is right, then everything else has a chance to work. "Create in me a pure heart, O God, and renew a steadfast spirit within me." *~Psalm 51:10 NIV*

The sermon, regardless of the length or style of delivery, has a chance to touch people's lives if coming from the preacher who is walking with God. The preacher is placed in the unique position of being able to connect others to Jesus through the spoken word.

No doubt, ill prepared sermons, with little content and poor delivery, will pour cold water on any worship service. All works together in the sermon. The person, the message and the method are all intrinsically woven into one. However, every preacher, regardless of how completely together he or she is, will preach sermons along the way that will not come across as hoped or intended.

The church that connects people to God will never have the problem of not having enough people. The mission of the church is to go out into the world and make disciples or connect others to God. "He said to them, Go into all the world and preach the gospel to all creation." ~*Mark 16:15 NIV*

"Therefore go and make disciples of all nations, baptizing them in the name of the Father and of the Son and of the Holy Spirit," ~*Matthew 28:19 NIV*

Chapter 3

Soul Winning in Any Community

A common expression today is, "We just can't reach the lost people in our community. We have tried and discovered it impossible."

If souls are to be saved, the attitude of "can't win them," has to be wiped away. I have discovered that persons can be won to Jesus Christ. It is possible for pastors and the passionate Christian to win the lost in any place.

Soul Winning is Essential

Soul winning is essential to the life of your church. If Sunday after Sunday is going by without the refreshing ordinance of baptism, your church may soon dry up and die.

Finding the Lost

Ask your people for names of the lost. If they look at you funny, ask for names of people who do not "belong to the church." I find that many Christians have not seen souls saved in such a long time that the terminology has changed. In other words, "church member" has been interchanged with the word "Christian" or "saved".

In some areas where I have preached, when asked about being a Christian people often reply "Yes, I belong to the church." This is a tragedy. If a person is just a church member, he has problems and the church will also have problems. People who are just church members are not interested in helping others to become Christians. Write down the names, phone numbers, physical addresses, email addresses and any other prospect information available. From this point you can begin to make personal contacts.

Another method of finding prospects is surveying. If you can recruit five or six people to help, you will usually find several prospects.

Reaching the Lost

If you are going to reach people today, you must create some interest. You must have something worthwhile happening. Something that makes people want to be a part.

Keep worship to about one hour. This does not mean that you are limiting the work of the Holy Spirit. It simply means you are using common sense. Some of your attendees won't mind going over an hour but you are trying to reach new people. New people will not want to be contained for much longer than an hour.

Work on your hour of worship. The service needs to flow and move. You can easily do twenty to twenty five minutes of music, prayer, scripture reading and even offer communion. You can then preach a good twenty to twenty five minute sermon and have a public altar call to receive Christ. You can have a good worship service in an hour or less. Pastors who arrogantly ignore this because they feel compelled to squeeze in their forty-five minute sermons are often fooling themselves. This is not a hard and fast rule. I preach in churches that often go up to two hours for worship. However, these cases are exceptions and not the norm.

Preach the Bible and make it relevant. There is so much going on in the world that preaching today cannot ignore current events. The Bible is as relevant today as ever before. Open the Bible and help people to find the way through Christ during today's murky times.

Winning the Lost

In the rural community, very few lost people attend church uninvited and then walk the aisle. One year, of the 51 additions we had, 31 were led to Christ through counseling in their homes or my office. Those who transferred their memberships had been approached and counseled before they ever came forward. I believe that one-on-one evangelism will produce fruitful results.

After getting the pertinent information about a prospect, you can then call or visit them. I like to call each prospect first. When I do, I explain to them who I am and then ask for an appointment. The plan is to meet at a specific time in the prospect's home or at the church. If you want to win persons to Christ, you need to be in a place where you can get and keep their attention. A pastor's office and church pew are both choice locations.

Too many pastors have attempted soul winning in front of the television or at a person's front door. A person may be driven further away if this method is used and it fails.

We live in a society of appointments. You will be more respected and you will appear more professional if you make appointments with the prospect. When an appointment is made, schedules can be cleared of things that might otherwise interrupt you. Unannounced visits to prospects do not usually produce the desired results. The visit or conference scheduled by both parties will usually prove most successful.

I have counseled with many people in my office. Many of whom prayed to receive Christ; others made a decision to move their letter to our church.

Many Who Have Not Heard

The longer I live, the more I discover people who have never heard the gospel. Over a span of three months, I once talked with fourteen people who admitted that they had never heard the plan of salvation. This same number had never seen a baptismal service. If I were in a remote section of the world, I would not think as much about such a response. But hearing people in the Midwest and Mideast say they have never seen a baptismal service is telling of the day in which we live.

How could anyone not have seen at least one baptismal service? One possibility is that pastors and churches have failed to do anything but sit on their theology. The majority have not tried to find the lost person. Rather, they have swept the idea under the rug and resigned themselves to just "ministering to the flock." Nothing is wrong with ministering to the flock, but failing to do anything to reach the lost is tragic.

Chapter 4

The Pastor's Role in the Church

People in small communities know the pastor. Even if they do not attend his church, his face and name become familiar to the community at large. The pastor is a central figure in the community. His position is important and meaningful to those who have day-to-day contact with him. Many different roles are conferred on the pastor. A pastor in a large city is different. The pastor of a church, in this setting, may feel that he is struggling for identity among the millions of people and thousands of other pastors in the city.

The church sees their pastor as shepherd. When I say shepherd, I mean the one who watches over the flock; who feeds the sheep; who counsels them when they are in need; and who visits them when sick or lonely. Many demands are placed on the pastor.

People often feel isolated from the world more than ever before. Homes have televisions, computers, cell phones, media devices of every kind, social networking, and internet sites. The list is almost endless. Yet, people feel estranged and unconnected from life and all the glamour that they think they are missing. People watch a lot of television and often compare their lives to those they view. A lot of people come to church wondering, "Where have I gone wrong? Why am I such a failure? What have I done wrong?" So, a pastor inevitably ministers to people with emotional problems that stem from feelings of failure, isolation and being disconnected from life.

Loneliness is another problem pastors must deal with. Pastors are often called upon to make visits to people in the church simply because these people are lonely. Throughout my ministry, I've enjoyed the friendship of many senior adults. Some of them were considered shut-ins because of health issues, age or possibly financial issues.

The pastor, who is visible in his community, will most likely have a successful ministry. I say successful because, if the people see him as being accessible, they will perceive him as a person who cares about people. People do not hesitate to share joys or problems with one whom they trust.

Another role of the pastor is that of healer. One of my former members was an 89 year old bedfast shut-in. This man was visited by a nurse about twice a month. However, I visited him weekly. We talked for a few minutes and had a prayer. His wife told me on several occasions how meaningful my visits were to them both and he shared with me how my visits helped him.

A 91 year old woman, with whom I visited regularly, often said "Your visits help me." Although she could get around some, she was seldom able to attend church. I do not fully understand what these people mean when they say my visits are meaningful and helpful. However, the visits seem therapeutic for them.

The pastor's prayer, offered beside a suffering saint is often soothing to that person's spirit. The touch of a pastor's hand is like the anointing of salve on a burn, it is healing. Yes, the congregation sees their pastor as a healer. Through him they are helped through bereavements, marital problems, sicknesses and spiritual problems.

However, a pastor can also be the recipient of that same kind of healing balm. When I left the bedside of a suffering saint, I was typically ministered to and helped even more so than the person in the bed.

Another role of the pastor is to allow (or compel) himself to be ministered to. A friend whom I called my "personal pastor" was with me when I learned that my Father had cancer. I was upset. After a few moments, he took me by the hand and said, "Let's pray." The prayer was almost like a sedative. I was greatly calmed and felt that some of the burden had been removed.

It is easy in the busyness of ministry to forget that the minister also has needs. If my prayers render any measure of strength and solace to others then I am certainly grateful. I know what they mean to me when friends have done the same.

Another role is that the pastor is often seen as a model. Everyone in town or the community eventually gets to know the preacher. Thus, the eyes of "everyone," at one time or another, seem fixed on him. If you require a great deal of privacy, pastoral ministry is not likely the place to find it. Everything you do should be done with that awareness.

This does not mean you can't be human, but it does mean that you have to be careful. People are watching to find out if you live what you proclaim from the pulpit. At first this might seem to be a horrible predicament. However, it can work to the pastor's benefit. The pastor has an opportunity to reveal Christ to others by example and not just words. The community thus becomes an extension of his ministry.

In the church, the pastor is looked to as a leader. My churches have responded to most every activity and program that I have planned and promoted. We sponsored many activities and special programs to promote the gospel. However, the congregations have looked to me, their pastor, to lead them in this area.

Prior to the beginning of one pastorate, the church had experienced only a few additions. After about six months of prayer and refocus, our people caught the spirit of seeing others come to Christ.

The pastor is often seen as a community leader. One of our community residents saw me on the street one day and asked, "What do you have planned next at the church?" In other words, she was looking to me to find out what programs I had planned for the congregation that might also benefit her.

The pastor's role in the church is that of a motivator. The pastor can motivate through preaching, writing letters of concern or appreciation to members, visiting, and by example. I stress "by example". If the people see the pastor involved in the program or project that is being promoted, they will be more apt to support it as well. A model is an effective motivator of people.

The final and very important role is that of prophet. The pulpit ministry of many churches, of today, is neglected. People come to the church on Sunday to hear a word from God. Unfortunately, some churches are dying because they are not hearing, "Thus saith the Lord." If a pastor fulfills all of the other functions and does not have a word from the Lord – failure is certain. Churches in rural as well as urban communities suffer if the pastor does not devote time to Bible study, prayer, and sermon preparation.

These areas do not cover the entire role of the local church pastor. But, generally speaking, if a pastor fulfills these roles, he will likely experience a successful and effective ministry.

Chapter 5

Pastoral Outreach

The marathoner cannot succeed without a strong commitment to reach the finish line. The ball player must commit to a regimen of daily exercise and strenuous practice. The concert pianist will go only as far as his commitment is to his instrument. The fisherman's success in bringing home a good catch for the day hinges on his commitment to a day of patiently casting and reeling.

The growing church is no different. Somewhere along the course of the church life, a strong commitment must be made to church growth.

The pastor plays the key role. His roles are not only in the realms of preaching, motivating, inspiring, organizing, leading, and teaching, but as importantly, in the realm of visiting. Several elements are important as the pastor leads in the realm of visitation.

Previous and Present Expectations

For almost forever, the pastor has been privileged, particularly in small towns and villages, to have the freedom to move about from door to door inviting people to church. In communities where this hospitality exists, the pastor can take advantage of it for making personal contacts. This century has brought change and transition. Many people resent cold calls and an uninvited visitor.

This open-door policy is nonexistent in urban areas. The pastor is a stranger. He is just one among the multitudes of people. The condominiums and apartments secured by private entrances prevent a pastor from having open access to the people living in them.

The Pastor's Compassion

At first, passion may seem out-of-place. But without passion, the pastor will not get the job of outreach and visitation accomplished. *Jude 1:22* says, "And of some have compassion, making a difference:" A burning passion for reaching people is essential for church growth. We must care. I believe that, before we can get the job done as pastors, a rekindling of compassion must occur in our lives.

As a child, I grew up on a lonesome mountain road called Milo. A creek runs past my home place. Across the creek are the remains of my grandparents' country store. I made several trips a day to see them since that was the focal point of my family's social life.

My mother had prayed fervently for my daddy's salvation. How I remember her regular Sunday morning question, "Are you going to church with me today?" The reply was usually, "No, I don't believe I will." My mother never gave up. One night while I was walking across the bridge from Grandpa's grocery, I heard crying on the front porch of our home. Walking up the concrete steps to the porch, I saw Mom and Dad embraced, weeping. I was frightened by it all.

An hour or so later, back in the house, I quietly asked Mother "What was happening out there?" With a sweet smile she replied, "Son, your daddy was saved tonight." "They that sow in tears shall reap in joy...bringing his sheaves with him." *~Psalm 126:5-6* Mother had a prayer life and passion for the salvation of her family.

If the pastor does not care much about reaching lost people for Christ, neither will the members. Pastoral visitation and outreach begin with compassion.

The Pastor's Personal Involvement

The pastor cannot escape outreach. You may be a great preacher. Good preaching is important. However, the pastor cannot grow a church just from the pulpit. He must be involved in daily outreach. This does not mean he does it all; but he is involved.

In a previous pastorate, our Bible study/Sunday school averaged about 400 contacts per week. Out of those 400, I made 40 to 50 of them per week. Some of these were by telephone, some in the hospital; many were in homes. Obviously, I did not do all of the outreach. I had the blessing of making some key visits that my church members and staff did not get in on.

Maybe you are able to get one good appointment per week. Yet, out of it someone makes a confession of faith or moves their membership to your church. You easily could net 52 additions to your church in one year.

One year, out of 48 baptisms, I met with most of the people one-on-one prior to the Sunday each joined our church. I must confess, I did not feel overworked or loaded down, but I did keep a weekly, steady pace of combing my prospect list and setting up appointments with those prospects.

From a negative viewpoint, if I had not been "beating the bushes," our church might only have had five-to-ten baptisms in a year. The pastor cannot do it all and should not try to do it all. However, the bulk of new members will come to fruition as a result of the pastor's labor.

Prospect Possibilities

Prospects are available. To obtain prospects try the following:

1. **Do a Sunday morning survey.** Pass a form out to your Sunday morning congregation for people to complete with names of prospects. They may list family members, neighbors, friends, or work associates. Even if only 50 people fill out one form, with only one name per form, you will have a tremendous log of names to follow up on.

2. **Do a Wednesday evening dialogue.** Write the names of the prospects on a chalkboard as the names are publicly called out. Prepare yourself for a full array of names. People are

inclined to call out several names, when they appear in writing, before the entire congregation.

3. **Do a survey of your in-house prospects.** Herein will be some people who have been waiting to talk to you. Sit down with your Sunday school/Bible study director, education director, or Sunday school workers. Comb the Sunday school roll for names of persons who have not made a profession of faith. I look for names of people who are in the fourth grade through senior adults.

Talk with people who work with your singles, youth, and children's programs. Your music program may also produce some prospects. All of the people have been attending and are ripe for decision.

You can delegate a lot of names. Your members can have a strong influence on your prospects. In working with your members you can see results.

The Pastor's Position

The office the pastor holds puts him in a logical setting to do the most effective visitation of any church member. The un-churched view the pastor as the spokesperson for his local congregation. The pastor's calls or visits to the prospect, about becoming a Christian or about transferring membership, are viewed as official.

Once I saw a district judge, from our town, out walking. I invited him to church. He visited with his family. He and his wife rededicated their lives to God during our altar time. He said he wanted to pray with me more about church membership. The next day, we sat in my study and talked for more than an hour about his life and desire to walk with God. This all began with a previous, informal encounter that led to a greater commitment on the part of his family.

The Pastor's Patience

This element of outreach may be the hardest one. You have seasons when you preach well, work hard, make a lot of visits, and nothing seems to happen. Our job is not to be successful, but to be faithful. If you are not making any efforts to reach people, you will not have church growth.

Even if you are trying by praying for and reaching out to prospects, you may not see any growth for some time. If you keep planting seeds and watering them, you will eventually have some harvest. If the seed is never planted, then growth never will occur.

Be patient. Stay committed to reaching people. Plant seeds by obtaining prospects' names and by cultivating relationships. Work hard with your staff and fellow church members by being partners. Ask God to give you a burden for reaching people. In time, with you as God's person at the helm of setting the pace, your church will grow.

Chapter 6

Doing Pastoral Care Through Preaching

Pastoral Care Involves Time

Pastoral care is a time-consuming part of ministry. Many churches seek pastors who have special skills in pastoral care. Once the pastor arrives on the field, he does not have to make announcements from the pulpit or purchase advertisements to gain the opportunity to do pastoral care. The folks who fill the pews are the same folks who will fill the pastor's study – and end up on his calendar.

These people often need a brief word from God about a problem or need comfort in the midst of crises. People enjoy hearing sermons that touch their lives. Most pastor search committees seek a man with good pastoral care abilities as well as effective pulpit abilities.

One pastor search committee chairperson told me that his church wanted certain characteristics in their new pastor. The two top items were: "A man who is a pulpiteer" and "one who has sufficient training in the area of pastoral care." This chairperson also said, "We have a great church; but we are a people, including myself, who, because of the condition of our world today need a pastor who can minister to our needs."

No doubt, other congregations feel the same way. Thus, a good deal of the pastor's time is taken up by ministry to people. One area of pastoral care that every minister will perform is that of hospital, convalescent center, and home visitation. This type of work will always exist.

Pastoral care is a valid ministry. The encouragement and help people receive from this service can never be fully appreciated by us until we are in the same situation - receiving pastoral care

from someone else. At times, this ministry may only take ten
to fifteen minutes per visit. Hopefully, it will involve words of
encouragement, and a prayer. This is truly pastoral care.

Another form of pastoral care is that which occurs in the pastor's
study or someone's home. In most cases the pastor is approached
for more than just a prayer. A church member may want to know
what God's Word says about grief, anger, or dealing with a marriage
problem. The person should not be satisfied with just a figure sitting
behind a desk. They want to hear something constructive about
whatever dilemma they are in.

The effective pastor listens to people's concerns before he speaks.
Thus, depending on the size of your church membership and
community, pastoral care can be a large share of your work week.

Killing Two Birds with One Stone

If more pastoral care was done from the pulpit, the need for office
and home sessions might not be as great.

For many years I conducted three worship services each week. I
like to have at least 24 hours per week to prepare for these special
hours. The time to prepare is important because the people who
attend are important. They deserve to hear a worthwhile sermon.

The typical congregation will be at least 80 percent church
members on Sunday morning, 95 percent on Sunday evening and
close to 100 percent on Wednesday evening. Our audiences are
overwhelmingly professing Christians and church members. During
these services, we have a great opportunity to minister to our people.
Each service will bring people to the church that have needs and are
inwardly crying for help.

How can we minister to these people? Do we preach about hell
every Sunday? Do we preach about the Roman road to salvation
every other Sunday? Most Christians would answer no, not because
they don't believe that lost people need to hear the plan of salvation

or because people should not be alarmed about the destination of the lost. Rather, they know the Lord Jesus and are convinced of their heavenly destination.

Yet, the people we face are a people with pressures, stress, domestic problems, and other needs that should be addressed. This does not mean that we forget the lost. Nor do we turn our attention away from prospects. However, it does mean that we take note of our audience when we begin to prepare our sermon.

In a previous pastorate, I tried to especially emphasize pastoral care in my own preaching. During this time, the church experienced twice the additions of previous years and three times the baptisms. Thus, it did not and should not hurt our evangelistic thrust.

Preaching and Pastoral Care

What does it mean to do pastoral care through preaching? It means teaching the Bible and a basic understanding about a human problem and ministering to the folks in the pews.

For example, I recently preached about depression. Two passages for this sermon are *Psalm 130:1*, "Out of the depths have I cried unto thee, O Lord."; and *1 Kings 19:4-7* where Elijah was depressed after his ordeal with the prophets of Baal and the threat from Jezebel that he "...went a day's journey into the wilderness, and came and sat down under a Juniper tree; and he requested for himself that he might die; and said, It is enough; now, O Lord, take away my life; for I am not better than my fathers".

Elijah was truly depressed. Yet the rest of this passage gives you some insight into Elijah's overcoming his depression. He rested, ate, and then did something else. He traveled to Horeb.

In this sermon, I talked about some things that might cause us to get depressed, noting Elijah's case. He was disappointed. He may have felt he had failed since Jezebel had scared him away. I also mentioned that a lack of something to do may have contributed to his depression. It was the end of an exciting time in his ministry. The battle on Mt. Carmel must have been especially exciting. This mountaintop experience was over, and he was not hungry and tired.

In this sermon, I discussed the physical, emotional, and spiritual side effects of depression. I then led the congregation in a prayer, reading what the psalmist wrote in *Psalm 130:1-5*, and encouraged them to meditate on his words. I then provided opportunity for response by giving an opportunity for people to come to the altar to pray.

After the service, at least 20 persons said in different ways, "Pastor, that sermon is just what I needed," or "Pastor, that sermon really spoke to me."

I felt good preaching that sermon. It was more than just a good sermon; it was 25 or 30 minutes of pastoral care. I shared with a large group of people, in a short segment of time, what it would take me weeks or months to do on a private or individual basis.

Preaching is a vehicle for doing pastoral care. It means always preaching in love and not using the pulpit as your Sunday whipping post. It means proclaiming God's Word with a caring heart and presenting Holy Scripture to people who are reaching out in a way that gives them something to grab on to.

Preaching About Life's Problems

A good plan of doing pastoral care from the pulpit is preaching a series of sermons about problems that might cause persons to seek counsel. Here are some ideas for your next sermons:

"Dealing with Stress"
"Accepting Yourself as God's Creation"
"Divorced, Now What?"
"Surviving Bereavement"
"Replacing Negativism with Positivism"
"Overcoming Loneliness"

"Handling Anger"
"Coping with Failure"
"Discovering Freedom from Guilt"
"When Parenting Gets Hard"
"Finding God's Will"
"Being at Peace with Your Life"
"Accepting Death with Victory"
"Getting Along with Parents"
"Making a Sour Marriage Work"
"When Your Children Disappoint You"
"Parenting Single-handedly"

These titles do not scratch the surface of sermon possibilities that might give pastoral care to your people.

Many people are not afraid to ask for the pastor's time. However, other people who need some form of pastoral care will never ask for it. The pastor who carries his pastoral care with him from the study to the pulpit will minister to both groups. This will give him more time to devote to this pulpit preparation.

Chapter 7

Ministry Headaches – Ministry Relief

Every job has its own set of problems. Whether the source of income is derived from a blue collar or white collar job, headaches of some kind are unavoidable. The pastor of a church also has his own share of headaches. I pastored several small churches in rural communities and felt positive about my ministry. Much of my life and church experiences developed in and around small town and rural community people.

Rural Commonality

Pastoring in rural communities and small towns allowed for a lot of beautiful moments in my life. For some, it might be stressful. Small communities abound with traditions and ideas that have been formed throughout generations of families. Thus, those living in the community often are reluctant to accept new ideas.

A person who enters such a community with unfamiliar ideas, especially if he attempts to impose those ideas on others, will likely not be very successful but will create problems for himself. It generally takes time and patience for people to adjust to new or different ideas. An impatient pastor will reap for himself more headaches than aspirin can cure. If, however, the pastor proves himself by labor and love and time spent on the field, he may witness gradual change.

Feeling of Fulfillment

Some pastors enter a rural area with visions of building a super church. With time, however, they realize the futility of such thinking. This does not mean that rural areas can't yield good and flourishing ministries. Pastors must understand that to compare a rural pastorate, with that of a big city church, is like trying to compare summer with winter. There are disadvantages to both. If a man understands this, he can come to derive his fulfillment needs from his achievements in relation to his congregation's possibilities.

I am reminded of Titus and his responsibilities on the Island of Crete. Crete was an undesirable place for a first century Christian to live. Paul said to Titus, "One of themselves, a prophet of their own, said, Cretans are always liars, evil beasts, idle gluttons." ~*Titus 1:12* For Titus, it may have seemed an unfulfilling place to live. But being the kind of person Titus was, he rolled up his sleeves and worked hard. He made the best of the situation. This is what every pastor should do regardless of the environment that surrounds him.

If every pastor would make the best of his "Crete," or his rural community, or whatever his situation, he will experience a sense of fulfillment. Fulfillment is a result of developing one's full potentialities. This realization doesn't come easily, but as a result of hard work.

Lack of fulfillment often generates hunger pangs for greener pastures. This hunger can be satisfied by two means; finding another place of service or making the present place enjoyable enough to stay. If you are in "Crete," try making the best of it for awhile. You will create your own success and happiness.

Peer Familiarity

In a small community, everybody gets to know you or know of you. In this environment, many pastors become "one of the crowd." This has its good points and offers ministry opportunities. However, it also has its drawbacks. A pastor can lose his identity as the shepherd. These areas of a pastor's discontent: rural commonality, un-fulfillment and peer familiarity, can lead to depression.

Depression

Depression is no respecter of persons. Pastors, as well as others, can become victims of its invasion. A pastor who is depressed may experience boredom and a feeling of hopelessness. He may feel far from God and even unworthy of being the shepherd of his flock.

Two methods that I use to overcome my depressive moments are lawn work and exercise. I joined a gym during one of my pastorates. It was a life saver. Whenever I get in a depressive state I get into my car and head straight for the gym. There, I can lift weights, swim, jog, or sit in a steam room. This brings up a good sweat and relieves a lot of stored tension. I always leave feeling better and refreshed. The membership also gives me an opportunity to meet people who are not members of my church.

Mowing the grass and gardening are good forms of exercise. They also relieve tension and promise a sense of well-being. One minister told me that his therapy is chopping wood. It's important to have methods of overcoming depression. If you don't, depression will overcome you.

If a person has succumbed to any or all of the pitfalls named thus far, they might well contribute to –

Family Pressure

When the husband's depression becomes apparent to the wife she becomes increasingly aware of any other problems her husband may be experiencing. She may then become concerned about two matters.

Stability – Pastors and their families usually move several times during their ministry. The moves sometimes are related to school or to changing positions. Moves are hard because each time it means pulling up roots and leaving friends. The adjustment period in any move is difficult. The pressure of feeling like the family has to move is excruciating for any family.

Security – It is not always easy to find another pastorate. When there is a feeling of pressure in the pastorate there is always the fear of security. Thus the question of, "How will we survive?" dwells in everyone's minds, especially if the pastor feels the problems are bad enough to warrant the consideration of moving.

Other Minor Aches and Pains

Everybody always knows what you are doing. If you are home, in your study, out of town, or visiting, people know about it. Privacy is not one of the benefits of the pastorate. This is something a person has to mentally adjust to if he is to get along with his people.

In a rural or small town setting most everybody knows about your finances. Most of the small communities where I served knew how much money I made. Since my salary was shown on the monthly financial report, it wasn't hard for anyone else to find out. Many people like to talk about how much money they make. The pastor who feels that his salary is a private matter often is in for some disappointment.

Pastoral headaches can get in the way of church growth. Pastors and church ministers must open their eyes to what they are doing. They are in the ministry. They are serving a church. They are doing God's work. Your work is totally dependent on God and His people.

If you can keep the small stuff small, then you can rise above it and provide the kind of leadership that your church needs in order to grow. If you let the headaches bog you down, then you will never have the heart that you need to lead your church to growth and greater effectiveness.

Elijah was having a great ministry. Preaching and experiencing the power of God in his ministry in a great way. As he faced the false prophet of Baal, God won the battle. Jezebel did not approve of Elijah's ministry and threatened him. Elijah ran for cover and became depressed unto death. Read the story in *1 Kings 18*. Elijah did what a lot of ministry leaders have to do. He got away and allowed God to bring him out of his depression. Sadly though, he allowed one wicked person to spoil his victory with God. God had handled the false prophets of Baal with fire from heaven. Eventually, He would take care of Jezebel as well as is documented in *~2 Kings 9:30-37*.

We have to trust our stress and headaches to God. God is greater than our every problem. There are those times that the evil nuisances of life seem to win. There are those moments when it seems that you have failed and are lost in your ministry. It seems that, maybe, God did not take care of you. Or, it seems that God let you down. When you have done the best that you can do and you are faithfully serving God, then He will make a way. It may not turn out like you had planned, but often God will work in your life in a greater way to bring greater glory to Himself.

Keep these factors in mind:
1. Your calling is from God. God called you into ministry.
2. God did not call you into ministry to abandon you.
3. God has everything that you need.
4. The church has some of the best people in the world.
5. The church has some of the meanest people in the world. Remember, it was a religious crowd that went after Jesus.
6. Look to God for His wisdom and direction in everything that you do.
7. Ministry work is the greatest work in the world. It is awesome to have a job that pays you to study God's Word and to do the work of God.
8. Enjoy every day. Get up each day with gratitude, joy and love. A good attitude is crucial.
9. Keep positive. Nothing in life is in concrete. Everything is

subject to change within a heartbeat.

10. If at first you don't succeed, try again. You may need to try in a different way. There are numerous ways to win the battle.

Chapter 8

How to Keep the Pastorate from Killing You

The church can seldom grow if the pastor and ministry leaders are dying on the inside. Some die altogether and go on to be with Jesus. But if the ministry leader is hurting inwardly it makes for an unhealthy church. Healthy churches are healthy from top to bottom. When the pastor is suffering it spills over into the congregation.

We have all seen churches grow even with pastors who were in different types of life crises. We are amazed that churches grow in these scenarios but they do. Usually, there is some kind of major trauma that will bring it all to a halt. The pastor breaks down, fails, falls short, quits, has a stroke, a heart attack or dies. When this happens, it will often bring the church to a place of questioning. "Why did this happen?" If not properly analyzed, the church will replace the pastor and may go through the same ministerial scenario within a few years. This continued kind of leadership trauma stymies the churches ability to ever reach its fullest potential.

Church leadership and pastors must talk about church and ministerial health. Healthy ministers are better able to oversee and tend to the flock. A flock that is overseen by a healthy shepherd has a better chance of going in the right direction.

The pastorate can have a great deal of stress and nerve-wracking moments. It is not unusual to read about a pastor's death, early retirement, or leaving the ministry for health related reasons.

Events, such as these, often occur because the pastor can experience a tremendous amount of stress and tense, day-to-day, unnerving situations before there is a calm or time of peace. Some pastors testify they never know a moment of peace.

One 40 year old pastor recently said, while sitting across the table from me at a meeting, "My church is killing me." I believe other pastors would admit to times when they have experienced the same feelings.

The pastorate is a different type of work. We may smile and agree with this statement; but the way we handle the uniqueness of our vocation is amazing. Sometimes we jump out of bed at dawn and immediately start going. Sometimes we are headed to the hospital or a meeting, while on other occasions we are just going. Some days this goes on all day long. At the end of the day, we feel as if we have been in the great race.

The pastorate requires wisdom and discipline. We must learn how to handle the number of hours we have each day. Some pastors have said, "You must get up early to study and pray." Well, this works great for some but not everyone. One pastor I know sleeps until 10:00 a.m. every day except Sunday. In the afternoons, he visits and takes care of other duties; from 9:00 p.m. until 1:00 a.m. he can be found studying and praying. His schedule is fine. He has been at this church for more than 10 years and the congregation has doubled in size.

The pastor's occupation is one that has been set apart. We have been called, by God, to a special task. Our job is not like the factory worker, the school teacher, or businessman. Our job is different from any other paid position on earth. Because of its difference and demands, our lifestyles must be different in order to keep the uniqueness of our high calling from killing us.

Suggestions That May Save You

Make your own schedule – This is a daily battle. As a pastor, it does not take long to make many acquaintances. So it is possible to have someone wanting some of your time every day. Some time ago we had friends from another town who called to say "We'll be up tomorrow for a couple of days." They kept their promise. We had so many things to do that we really did not need someone to entertain. They made our schedule for us for three days. I love people and enjoy having people in my home. However, it works better for everyone if it is put on the calendar for everyone's convenience.

Every pastor will have church members call and request his presence and his time. Keep a calendar. If something is already scheduled, say so. It will give you peace of mind. Besides, people sense when you are squeezing them into your busy schedule.

Realize your humanity – You are not a machine. Your body demands rest. You cannot do everything single-handedly. Many of us seem to forget that we are not superhuman or made of iron. We are flesh and bone.

Our humanity is sometimes a hard pill to swallow. Often, we fail. We preach a sermon that was not as effective as we would have liked or we are unable to accomplish all that we feel needs to be done in our daily routine of Christian service.

Do the human things – The wedding Jesus attended at Cana was certainly a social outing. It shows us something of the humanity of our Lord. He was truly human; He did human things. Human beings must do human things.

It is inspirational to hear about great men of God who pray all day or who walk the streets searching for lost souls. Yet, I was inspired when I heard a pastor admit the other day that he enjoyed riding a motorcycle, playing golf, and shooting a pistol for recreation. These are human things. We are human beings. Until we die, our minds and bodies have a basic need for the human things.

This basic need should be fulfilled in two areas: personal time and family time. Every pastor needs time to be alone, and every pastor needs to be with his family. I've heard too many pastors express regrets such as "I wish I had not been so busy while my children were growing up." This goes back to managing our schedules. We must make time for our family, and we must make time for ourselves.

I can hear a frustrated pastor saying "I don't have the time for such noble causes." Take the time. You are worth it; your family is worth the time. Your church deserves it.

Cultivate friendships – During a period in my ministry, I felt that I did not have many friends. It is a bad feeling, but I soon realized that I had not taken time to cultivate any friendships. I had many acquaintances but was not that close to very many people.

Other pastors can be good friends. We understand each other. We can relate to one another's daily routines. We can empathize in the hard times and rejoice in the good times. Pastors need to get together for lunch or to participate in some type of recreation – anything which builds relationships.

Neighbors make good friends. How much does it cost to bake a cake or make coffee? Invite some of your neighbors over from time to time.

Church members can be good friends. I am not suggesting that you divulge every frustration in your life to those you serve. They can be friends but rarely can they be someone you pour your heart out to. You will only have one or two of those kinds of friends along the way. Normally, they are not people who help pay your salary. However, some of my better friends have been people that I have served.

The relationships I have with some have taken two or three years to develop, but I can let my hair down with them. They accept me as I am. Making friends with church members takes wisdom and cultivation. Some church members can be nothing to you other than members. It takes time to find those with whom you can relate and relax.

I can hear someone saying, "If I followed through on these suggestions my church would fire me." No, the members will respect you more. They will begin to see you as a person instead of some transcendent being called "Pastor." They may even give you a raise!

Do not allow God's calling to become your death. Let it be your life.

Chapter 9

Church Agents - Helping the Church Grow Together

Leadership team members, deacons or elders play a major role in church growth. Because of this major role, their activities can be a great help or great hindrance. Many times, their role either promotes or demotes growth. It is essential that the agents of church leadership be agents of positivism, and Christian example if growth is to occur.

Agents of Positivism

In some churches, the deacons or elders screen everything before it is put into action. This can be a major tragedy, especially if these leaders are negative about everything or anything new. However, if the leadership agents are open-minded and willing to be positive about a Bible study emphasis, discipleship program, outreach effort or whatever the need is, then a church is more likely to experience growth.

Many churches have become stagnant because of the attitude – We've never done it this way before. Or, we've done it this way for 50 years, and it's still good enough for me. Or, as one old country gentleman once said, "My grandfather did it this way, and that's good enough for me." If the leadership agents take on this close-minded spirit, the church will not experience growth; they will experience decline.

The church must constantly seek ways to win people to Christ, do mission work, increase attendance and giving. Thus, the leadership agents are responsible for being open to new methods that might produce results and reach people.

Agents of Service

Many churches have leaders who do nothing but serve as board
members. A person should never accept a church leadership
position with the idea of just sitting around a table and making
decisions. A church with nonworking leaders can experience
only limited growth. The congregation expects those serving in
leadership positions to visit, call on the sick, be available to minister
at nursing homes and funerals, and to help the needy. A church
whose agents do not take Christian service seriously will be limited
in growth.

Agents of Harmony

The peacemakers of the church are those who serve as leaders.
Whenever a squabble among members begins to affect the welfare
of the church, these appointed leaders must go to work. Unresolved
difficulties and hard feelings will hinder the moving of God's spirit.
Growth is not possible in this kind of environment. In many
churches, everyone knows what the other person is doing. When
there are problems, in the church, it gets around and thus kills the
interest of prospective members. Leadership agents must be able
to solve problems in order for the church to experience growth. A
harmonious church is a healthy church. Healthy churches can grow.

Agents of Outreach

Christians look to the elders, deacons, leadership team and pastor
to lead in outreach. If the pastor and leaders will not visit, then no
one else will visit. One woman once said, "Our deacons rarely show
up for visitation, why should I?" I do not agree with her reasoning.
Chances are she would not participate in the outreach program even
if the deacons did. However, when the deacons do not participate
they hurt the program of outreach. Because of their place of
acceptance in the community, deacons in most churches could

probably win more people to Christ than the pastor.

Agents of Christian Example

Christian people are looking for models. The pastor is not enough. He is often a stranger brought in from another place. The people often take his work for granted and say, "The pastor is supposed to do such and such, because he receives a salary." But deacons, elders and other elected or appointed leaders are often pillars of the community. They have grown up among the people and thus are known. If the leadership agents attend and support the work of the church, then so will many of the other people. If the leadership agents take the church lightly, then so will everyone else. These special church agents must be examples of Christian living. This example can mean much to the growth and ministry of the church.

Trustees, deacons, elders, leadership team, minister...however named in your church, each has the responsibility and privilege to be God's agent of growth in your community.

Chapter 10

Growing and Ministering Through Bible Study

The Sunday school is a great organization for reaching new people. A number of churches still do not have Sunday schools and have elected to have small Bible study groups that meet throughout the week. Either will work. In most cases, the Sunday morning Bible study group that meets at the church before worship seems to be the most consistent form of small Bible study groups.

One church I served grew in attendance and in membership by virtue of the Sunday school. This organization was responsible for higher attendance and for outreach to people we otherwise might never have reached. This congregation averaged about 100 to 150 in Sunday school. This attendance changed to 250 to 300 in attendance when the Sunday School Council, Sunday school director, and pastor began to meet regularly. In these meetings, important things happened that affected the course of our Sunday school.

Prayer was foremost. Each department director, the Sunday school director and the pastor began to pray. These prayers were for wisdom concerning the Sunday school and for God's guidance in making our organization a better one. When we forget to pray, we are overlooking our greatest source of power. It is through prayer that we know the mind of God and learn His perfect will.

Proven principles were outlined. The principles we emphasized were to enlist and train new workers; to enlarge the Sunday school organization; to provide space for new classes to meet and to get prospects enrolled in Sunday school.

This is a key point in either failure or success. Every Sunday school should have an active council or leadership team. This council or leadership team should consist of division directors, department directors, the outreach director, the Sunday school / Bible study director, the pastor, the minister of education (if a church has one) and other general officers. This group should meet monthly.

Planning was implemented. One of the basics of growth is to start new classes. A new class takes on the spirit of a mission-type endeavor. The teacher and other leaders normally have a "let's go" spirit about them. A new unit has empty chairs and space to fill. Thus, the new unit takes on a spirit of outreach to fill its space. The teacher and members assigned to the class begin to ask, "Who do I know that might be a prospect for my class?"

Purpose is essential in planning. Starting a new unit is fine, but the best action is to have a purpose for this new class. The new units we started were for the purpose of reaching people. A special education class was formed. A unit especially designed for reaching those with mental handicaps provided a great opportunity for ministry.

Single adults were another group on which we focused. A department grew out of this emphasis. A class or department that provides weekly Bible study and fellowship could largely increase the attendance. In general, enlarge your organization, and you will increase your attendance.

Providing space is essential. The church, at that time, was probably one of the few in our area that did not have Sunday school rooms. We had a sanctuary, a fellowship hall and a balcony. Yet we had more than 300 on a good day in Sunday school and averaged more than 260 my second year in weekly attendance. This result occurred by utilizing our space to the limit.

We had partitions everywhere. We used our kitchen and baptismal dressing rooms for classroom space. Our fellowship hall was used by many classes as well. The next step was to provide more space for more growth. The next year, the church was able to purchase a building that was next door for additional classroom space.

People attend when they are contacted. Our Sunday school grew because we averaged 20 to 35 people visiting every Thursday night. Each Thursday, a particular department sponsored visitation. We met at 7:00 p.m. for prayer and assignments and teamed up to make outreach contacts to people.

Please note that these were not normally evangelism visits. These visits were typically a knock on the door to say hello and to invite the person to Bible study and church. Occasionally, there was an opportunity to share the gospel. Normally, an effort to lead someone to Christ was more successful when an appointment with the candidate was made.

We then would come back at 8:30 for refreshments and reports. The fellowship, refreshments and reports seem to be a plus for bringing people out to participate in our weekly visitation program.

Prayer, proven principles, planning, purpose, providing space, and people are the P's that will help your Sunday school/Bible study ministry grow and minister to many more people.

Chapter 11

Growing the Bible Study Program

Growth is Possible

Church Bible study growth is possible, whether the church setting
is rural, small town or large city. We all like potential. We look at
communities and speak of areas that have great potential. Every
area has potential. Most churches will never have an attendance of
several hundred. The majority of churches across America average
less than a hundred people on Sunday. However, one rural church
that is in the middle of a horse field in Kentucky has grown from
30 to an average of 800 to over 900 on most Sundays. People drive
from as far as 30 miles to attend. Over the last ten years they have
developed an exciting ministry that includes Bible study, preaching,
music and a place that people enjoy attending.

The pastor is the key to awakening people to the possibility
of growth. If the pastor does not see the possibilities, then his
congregation never will. The pastor is the shepherd and, thus,
becomes central in helping his flock catch the vision. But if
he never sees it, he will not be able to lead his members in that
direction. Pastors must realize and see the possibilities of using the
small groups or Sunday school to grow the church.

Your church may be able to grow from 30 to 50 or from 150 to
5000. Whatever your potential, growth in your Bible study program
is possible.

Emphasize the Bible

The Sunday school or small group's first task is to teach God's
Word and lead persons to apply that learning to life.

Unfortunately, some churches have Sunday school only for children. In previous pastorates, our attendance began to increase when we promoted Bible study. During the services, I would often emphasize what Bible book youth and adults were studying. This emphasis on the Bible seemed to increase interest in Sunday school.

Many people are interested in learning more about the Bible. When Bible study is emphasized people will respond and participate.

Provide Opportunities for All People

I once pastored a rural church that had a grand total of two Sunday school classes, with a total of 25 persons in attendance. After being at the church for awhile, I suggested that we double our number of classes. Members agreed to the suggestions and church leaders enlisted more teachers. Soon our attendance increased to 41. New classes will grow faster than older ones.

Churches must create classes or small groups to reach people. A class or group for every age group is essential.

Set Goals

Many churches maintain about the same attendance year after year. They become content with this average and never hope for anything greater. The writer of Proverbs says, "Where there is no vision, the people perish." ~*Proverbs 29:18*

Some Sunday schools are suffering today because they have no vision. They just want to maintain what they have. An insurance salesman once told me that his business never amounted to anything until he began to set goals. When he set goals, his business doubled. In striving to reach a goal, he became successful.

If your Sunday school is averaging 75 in attendance and dares to work for 150, on a given day, you may only have 110 people, but that does not mean that you failed. Rather, you discovered 35 more people who can be in your Sunday school.

Set goals and strive to reach them. Growth will occur even if you do not reach a particular goal.

Regular Workers' Meetings

Many churches never have regular workers' meetings. Lack of planning contributes to a failing or dying Sunday school. Small rural Sunday schools need weekly workers' meetings, if not once a week, then at least once a month.

During this meeting, lessons should be planned and activities for the month reviewed. Discouraged teachers should be motivated and good work recognized. The Bible study program will take on added importance.

A Sunday school/weekly Bible study program can grow in any community. The pastor is the key.

Chapter 12

Sunday School and Ministry

Involving the Bible study in ministry comes through leading each class or Bible study unit to understand its ministry potential. Thus, ministry is facilitated by a well organized, age graded Sunday school.

When I moved to one pastorate, all the men from 21 thru 93 years of age were meeting together. This grouping of ages was not working to anyone's advantage. This class was divided into four groups which provided our Sunday school an opportunity to meet the needs of adults at every age level.

For each class to realize that it is a small unit within the church, the teacher must realize his or her importance. The teacher's role is not just being the teacher, but also being the leader, or "pastor" of the group.

A good teacher demonstrates concern for each person, works to keep the class together, and leads members to help the class grow spiritually and numerically. Each class member has certain needs, and the teacher is in a strategic position to minister to those needs and to involve other members in ministry.

Togetherness Enhances Ministry

The ministering Bible study work, of the church, is one made up of classes and departments that do many things together.

1. **Study the Bible** – In the classroom or at home, class members become more likely to minister to one another and persons beyond the class because they study the Word together each week.

2. **Pray** – Members pray together for each other, the church,

the pastor, and persons who are not members but have needs.

3. **Work** – Members of the group make telephone calls, send emails, write letters, send cards, or make visits to absentees and prospects.

4. **Reach Out** – If every class, under the leadership of its teacher, will focus on the unsaved individuals and families in its age group, the Sunday school and church will grow dramatically.

Fifteen Sunday school teachers leading their classes to pinpoint, pray for, and win lost souls for Christ, will make a greater impact on the church than one person, the pastor, trying to do the work alone.

The Class Helping the Church

Classes and departments that minister effectively to members will add to the general life and welfare of the church. When each class functions effectively, members develop love for one another. Persons will want to attend Sunday school because they know they are loved and that they belong. Sunday school becomes meaningful to them.

When classes fail to reach out and minister to human needs, the entire Sunday school organization is affected. When the Sunday school organization is not vital, the entire church is affected.

A caring, ministering spirit can be enhanced by class fellowships. Often, classes in our church get together for recreation, a meal, a trip, or a prayer meeting in homes. As a result, Sunday school becomes an additional opportunity to strengthen fellowship and ministry to members and to nonmembers.

Ministry Ideas that Work

Classes must recognize how helping lost persons contributes to reaching them for Christ.

A monthly collection for a food basket is a specific ministry idea to consider. If six to ten class members bring one or two nonperishable items each Sunday, then once a month they can give assistance to an individual or family in the name of the Lord. Other ways classes can help are by providing clothing; driving someone to the grocery store, shopping mall, or doctor's office; or making a repair on someone's home.

A Young Adult class might want to help a young couple with a need, whereas a Senior Adult class might join together to help a senior adult. Each class can minister to those persons within its age group but should not be limited by age groupings. Whenever ministry is performed, persons are touched by God's love and may be led closer to enrolling in Sunday school and accepting Christ as Savior.

Every Sunday school can become involved in ministry when each class or department realizes its potential in ministering to members and nonmembers alike. The result will be winning persons to Christ and growing the church.

Chapter 13

Training Workers in the Small Sunday School

Few, small Sunday schools, are fortunate enough to have a seminary-trained Minister of Education. Normally, most cannot even begin to compare with the resources of leadership, personnel, or financial undergirding enjoyed by many large Sunday schools. However, small Sunday schools can have effective training.

Promoting Training

An old saying is, "You can lead a horse to water but you can't make him drink." If the horse is thirsty, he will drink. Sunday school workers also must become thirsty or Sunday school training will be meaningless.

Leaders can help create a thirst by leading workers to become interested in training. Communication is the key to creating this thirst. Fortunately, the small Sunday school has three methods that it can strategically use.

1. **Paper-newsletter communication** – Every church should have a weekly bulletin that has space for scheduled events. This space is a valuable tool. Here, the pastor can mention upcoming meetings and training sessions. People read the bulletin on Sunday mornings. List in the bulletin what is important. The bulletin is a good place to get the attention of workers.

   Another way to develop a thirst for training is through personal letters. I write to Sunday school workers often, encouraging them to take advantage of meetings. Emphasizing the importance of their jobs makes workers more conscientious about attending training sessions. People still love receiving a letter in the mail. However, because of time, ease and cost, most of the letter writing has become email, instant messages and text messages. Email/Web site and other Internet forms of media – Most likely the day will come when all church newsletters in paper form will cease to exist. Every church must develop a good email list of members and keep them updated. Every church must have a maintained web site.

2. **Pulpit communication** – If a pastor will occasionally tie training or teaching improvement ideas into a sermon, he will convey his belief that trained workers are important. Sometimes, workers do not see the importance because the pastor does not appear to be concerned about training.

3. **Personal communication** – If the pastor can find two or three helpers, then personal contact is unbeatable. A personal phone call from the Sunday school/Bible study director or pastor will let workers know that the session is important.

Providing Training

Every Sunday school has resources for training. Normally, the pastor is the key resource. He is the leader who is often familiar with the best and most recent study material and teaching approaches. Often, he is in a key position to equip teachers and to develop and equip leaders. A good pastor will equip several leaders and then work with them to accomplish the task of training.

We also learn by visiting other Bible study programs. Contact a pastor from another community, a pastor whose Sunday school or weekly Bible study program has experienced success in growth, training and organization. Take some of your people to see what they are doing. Schedule a meeting with the pastor and some of the leaders and hear from them on what they are doing that has been successful.

Or, If possible, have his Sunday school workers come to your church over a period of time and meet with some of your leaders and workers. Your Sunday school will be helped, encouraged, and stimulated. Being around other workers who enjoy their roles and are experiencing success will help your workers. Your Sunday school will improve.

If you do not have trained Sunday school workers, it is not because you cannot have them. Trained workers can be a reality in your Sunday school. Move forward with better trained and equipped Bible study teachers and leaders.

Chapter 14

The Small Church Syndrome - Overcoming It

I pastored four very small churches. I began pastoring rural churches as a high school student and did so through my seminary training. During this period I observed three defeatist attitudes sometimes present in churches, whether rural or urban.

We're Small and We Like It

Many churches have been small in number for so long that they are proud of their size. Because of this joy over their small membership, they often work harder to keep it small than to improve their attendance.

I recall pastoring a church when I first began seminary. Their Sunday attendance was averaging about 45. I challenged the people to aim for an attendance of 100 on a given Sunday and with much promotion we had 122 present. It was a great victory for many of us in the church. Unfortunately, several of the members did not like the big increase. One lady said in a complaining tone, "Well, I don't have to have all these people to worship the Lord." A man gruffed, "I couldn't find a place to sit down today."

I agree, I can worship by myself as far as numbers are concerned, but it certainly makes attending church a little sweeter with the pews filled with people. And, praise the Lord if I have trouble finding a seat.

If your church is stuck in the syndrome of "small and loving it", your church can be delivered from this syndrome with the help of three types of people.

  1. The Church Member Who Cares – Look around you and

take note. Who are the people in your church who thirst
for growth? Who are those who are dry from not seeing the
satisfying ordinance of baptism? If your church is in the
"small and loving it" syndrome there will not be many of
these people.

I cannot guarantee anything, but in the small churches
that I've pastored, God always seemed to provide some who
desired to reach out to people even as I did. These people
always helped because they understood my feelings. They
were strengths, because they usually had names of prospects
and they were ready to visit them or lift them up in prayer.
The pastor of members who desire to break the barrier of
"We're small and we like it" must seek out those who would
like to experience growth.

2. **The New Member Coming into the Fellowship** – One
   problem with many small churches today is the same people,
   who, for so many years have performed the same jobs. They
   have performed them in the same way, and are unwilling to
   make any changes. What is the church to do? Continue
   forever until it dies of staleness? We should work to assist
   those who themselves are willing to change and who will
   attempt to wake up those who are asleep in the church.
   Many small churches need some new blood. They need
   to be willing to try new ideas to reach those in their area.
   New members may be new converts. Or, they may be those
   who live in the community that need to move their letter
   to your church, or persons who have recently moved to the
   community. These additions will bring a freshness to your
   church.

3. **The Dedicated Pastor** – The pastor is the key to helping
   small churches become larger ones. The pastor must have
   a burden to see positive changes take place and he must be

willing to work to bring them about.

We Can't Do Any Better

The second observation I have made is that an attitude of "We can't do any better" is often reflected in their growth, or lack of growth.

I remember working in a small mission church. It had been a mission for about 15 years and still had the same number of people as when it started. After working in the field with them for several months, I discovered why they had the attitude of "We can't do any better." The reason they couldn't was because they really didn't want to.

The pastor and key leaders within the church are essential in changing this attitude. Upon coming to this church, I was faced with staggering statistics. The five years which preceded my coming had been a time of baptismal dryness. Only a handful of people had been baptized. The year immediately before, no one had been baptized. During my first year, while praying, preaching and searching prospects, we baptized 25 new converts. This generated a positive attitude.

Not only did we get our baptistery wet, the people began to give. In a period of one year, we bought and paid cash for a new Allen organ; black topped our church parking lot and paid the full amount upon its completion; and set aside a scholarship assistance fund that would be annually awarded to a qualifying, graduating senior. Then, to top it off, they gave me a fifteen percent raise. To a large church these are meager accomplishments. But to our small church, they were evidences of the convictions of rededicated Christians and the outpouring of God's blessings.

The people began to believe that they could, by God's grace, do anything. Our attendance increased from 50-60 to 120-150. We had a more positive outlook as a congregation.

The Hokey Syndrome

The third aspect is hokey. I have visited and preached in a couple of hokey churches. While I have preached in many, many great churches, I have preached in two or three that fit the hokey criteria. These are the situations that encourage some to make light of churches. What I mean when I say hokey is the following:

1. Not having any semblance of an order of service. Even if you do not have bulletins, there needs to be some order of service.

2. "Special" music provided by someone who never rehearsed their presentation. It did not sound very good.

3. A sermon prepared by the letter method. Just open your mouth and "let-ter" fly. These sermons normally go on forever with the pastor trying to figure out something to say.

4. Children constantly pacing the floor. They distract the attention of those attempting to worship. I have been in a few churches where the adults were as bad as the children.

5. Beginning late. It is very hokey to start a service 10 minutes late.

6. Running in and out of the sanctuary. I have attended some services where people get up and leave and then return to their pew two or three times.

These things contribute to a carnival or hokey atmosphere in a worship service. A little time spent in planning could correct much of this problem. You will find that having some order in the service will make your worship more meaningful and more harmonious.

Good music is vital to the worship service. We live in a music world. Today, every church can have a praise team, praise ensemble, musicians and a good choir. Although it takes work to pull it together, the singers and musicians are out there. They are hungry to serve God and to be useful. Do not allow just anyone to sing solos. Some can and some cannot. If they can't sing it is better to forego the music than to have bad music. Good music helps to prepare one for worship. Make sure your choir, praise group or soloist is prepared.

There is seldom an excuse for an unprepared sermon. Make sure you set aside time to prepare your sermon. Those who say something in the pulpit on Sunday worth hearing have usually thought and lived it during the week.

Small children need to be under close supervision during the worship. A church pastor or leader can salvage his time of worship by finding good leadership for children's worship and nursery care during the worship hour. This benefits everyone. The children benefit as well as the parents and church.

Beginning on time indicates that you do not wish to waste your time or the congregation's time. Let's face it, when 12:00 noon rolls around you have usually lost the ear of your congregation.

If you use bulletins, tactfully insert a message asking people to refrain from walking in and out of the sanctuary. If you do not have bulletins, you, as the pastor or leader, should explain from the pulpit, how moving about disrupts the service. Encourage them to remain in their places until the service is over, if possible. Let's face reality, anyone might have to leave the worship service briefly, but if they are going to have to leave again it is better to stay outside the worship service rather than disrupting it.

Finally, ask everybody to turn off their electronic devices. Surely we can give God our full attention for worship. Put the texts, email and calls on hold. Nothing interrupts anymore than a cell phone going off in church or the sound of someone texting. It has happened to me. While I was preaching my cell phone went off one time. It's an interruption that we can avoid.

Regardless of the size of your church you can maintain a certain amount of dignity and order. Be proud of your church. No matter if you have ten or a thousand in attendance, show respect for your church. The hokey syndrome will be overcome when a pastor and other church leaders desire the best for the congregation. The congregation will do and perform only as its leadership encourages and sets the example. The example of doing things right and to the best of one's ability is the beginning of progress.

Chapter 15

Don't Get Stuck

The seven deadly words of any organization are, We've Never Done It This Way Before. Everyone likes routine and tradition. Change, for change sake, is rarely effective. However, churches, pastors, ministries that grow have to try new methods and ideas. Our message of Christ remains the same, but new methods will always be unfolding.

Do not be afraid to change directions. If something doesn't work, then try something different. Churches copy what other churches are doing. Sometimes this is effective and sometimes it is not. Be attentive to what God is leading you and your church to do. Follow your heart. Let God lead you.

Churches get stuck - same ministry, same routine, mired in tradition. The church has to stay fresh. We must try new ideas, new approaches and new programs. Be creative in all ministries whether it is children, youth, or senior adults. It is about reaching people for Jesus.

"Yet you, Lord, are our Father. We are the clay, You our potter; we are the work of Your hand." *~Isaiah 64:8 NIV*

God is the potter and we are the clay. God molds us and uses us in different ways. Everyone starts out as an original and then ends up very similar to someone else. We have our favorite church, whether we attend it or not. We have our favorite preachers and teachers. We have mentors that we love and admire. Anyone who grew up listening to Billy Graham would start sounding a little bit like him occasionally. There is nothing wrong in sounding a little bit like a great preacher. It is better to sound like a great preacher than to sound like a not so great preacher.

Churches that are attempting new ministries are better to copy a successful church and ministry than to try programs that have failed everywhere else.

In many cases, churches will have some success with a ministry or program, but then, continue the program long after it should have closed or been buried. Some of the work we do is seasonal. It works for awhile, then we need to move on to something else.

We need to pray and seek God's direction. He is the potter. He can work with, through and in our lives and ministries if we will give him the opportunity.

God calls us to do different jobs and tasks. Paul gives us an excellent lesson on this in *1 Corinthians 12:12* For the body is not one member, but many. All persons bring different gifts and functions to the church. Every part of the body is not an eye, ear or hand. We have different talents and gifts and all these together make up the body of Christ. All members have different roles in the church. All parts of the body have different functions.

The church that allows the potter to take the members of the body of Christ and mold them to be the people He wants them to be will be a healthier church and will attract others to join them. The church that allows God to be the potter and to break and remold them as He deems necessary, from time to time, will experience life and freshness in its ministry. The church or ministry that becomes stuck or stale, and unwilling to spend time listening to God, will soon gravitate in the wrong direction. More than ever before, there are "For Sale" signs on church buildings across America.

The Bible says, "Trust in the Lord with all thine heart; and lean not unto thine own understanding. In all thy ways acknowledge Him, and He shall direct thy paths." *~Proverbs 3:5-6*

"In their hearts humans plan their course, But the Lord establishes their steps." *~Proverbs 16:9 NIV* God directs our steps.

- **Keep Praying.** A church that continues to pray fervently can receive fresh leading from God.
- **Stay in God's Word.** You will not go the wrong way reading the right book. God's Word is the lamp unto your feet and a light to your path. *~Psalm 119:105*
- **Be Obedient.** As God leads you, follow what He is telling you to do. Jesus said in *John 10:27* "My sheep hear My voice, and I know them, and they follow me:"
- **Be Humble.** We are all dependent on God. The Bible says, "Pride goeth before destruction, and an haughty spirit before a fall." *~Proverbs 16:18* God is the one who provides the blessings. Showers of blessings come from above.
- **Be Flexible.** Change is always all around us. As we pray, listen and respond, God is working, molding and providing opportunities for us to do His work. He leads us as we are willing to follow Him. *Isaiah 30:21* says, "Whether you turn to the right or to the left, your ears will hear a voice behind you, saying this is the way; walk in it."

Love God – The very best we can do is to keep our love relationship fresh with God.

As we pray, read God's Word and walk daily with Him, we cannot keep from growing in our love for Him. We have *1 Corinthians 12* where Paul gives us the excellent chapter on the body of Christ and the gifts of the members of the body. Then he ends chapter twelve, heading to chapter thirteen saying, "…And yet I will show you the most excellent way," *~1 Corinthians 12:31 NIV*, pointing to love as the most indispensable gift of all. In chapter thirteen, we have the Bible's beautiful love chapter.

All of our church work, ministry, service, preaching, teaching and giving must be centered in the love of God. It is about our love for Jesus. If we do not love Jesus, then our work is a like a clanging cymbal. The substance of all that we say and do must be Christ-centered and based on our love for Him and the love that we have been shown by Him to us.

If the work of your church, your preaching, teaching or any aspect of your ministry is suffering, then first spend time walking with God and loving Him. Reach out to God in love as God is always reaching out to us in love. Love always makes the difference. "... love covers a multitude of sins." ~1 Peter 4.8 NIV

God loves us and we love Him. God loves the world and wants to love people through us. This is the heart of our ministry and our Christian service. If all of our programs, ministries and work have, at their core, the love of God and our love for Him, there will never be a feeling of staleness. The love of God brings power to the church and to everyone who serves Him.

Lightning Source UK Ltd.
Milton Keynes UK
UKHW01f0623280618
324919UK00002B/596/P